Looking for Light from the Dark Side of the Moon

G ORDON L E WELL; K ATHRYN P ARKER

Order this book online at www.trafford.com
or email orders@trafford.com

Most Trafford titles are also available at major online book retailers.

Print information available on the last page.

ISBN: 978-1-4907-6529-7 (sc)
ISBN: 978-1-4907-6530-3 (hc)
ISBN: 978-1-4907-6537-2 (e)

Library of Congress Control Number: 2015915456

Because of the dynamic nature of the Internet, any web addresses or links contained in
this book may have changed since publication and may no longer be valid. The views
expressed in this work are solely those of the author and do not necessarily reflect the
views of the publisher, and the publisher hereby disclaims any responsibility for them.

Any people depicted in stock imagery provided by Thinkstock are models,
and such images are being used for illustrative purposes only.
Certain stock imagery © Thinkstock.

Trafford rev. 09/22/2015

www.trafford.com
North America & international
toll-free: 1 888 232 4444 (USA & Canada)
fax: 812 355 4082

G.L. EWELL

Engineer Castle

Also by Kathryn Parker

REFLECTIONS OF THE
POETIC MUSE
(written under the pen name of Katie E Parker)

POETRY WITHIN THE
SETTING SUN

"These poems are dedicated to anyone who has ever truly been in love. To those of us who have felt their breath catch from the warmth of a loved one's glance. Where happiness seemed like a second language, passion and desire, it's first. For those of us who have heard a song playing in our souls that was meant only for them, may these words touch our hearts, bring us a smile, and help us to remember that at one time life was a very beautiful thing."

—Kathryn Parker

"For everyone who could use a smile, a laugh, or just a good feeling in your heart; knowing that you are not alone in your joy, happiness, hardships, trials, or pain as you travel through this journey we call 'Life.'"

—Gordon Ewell

G.L. EWELL

Wings of Love

Contents

Section One
Poems By Kathryn Parker

Section Two
Poems By Gordon L. Ewell

Section Three
"GORDY-ISMS"

Random thoughts, comments and quotes collected from the "Post War" mind of recovering author Gordon L Ewell. Little "snippets" meant to give you a laugh, a smile, or just something to ponder and think about as you go about your day to day routine. Each of them is original, by author Gordon L Ewell, unless otherwise noted.

List of Illustrations
Illustrated by Gordon L Ewell

The illustrations are listed in the order they appear in the book. Listed first is the name of the illustration, then is the section it is associated with or page number.

Preface

Few are those who see with their own eyes and feel with their own hearts.

—Albert Einstein

Poetry is nothing more than art in motion via the written word. It is a way of connecting with someone feelings of joy, sorrow, tragedy, triumph, failure and victory, of hope and faith.

It is giving a gift of thought, a piece of your own heart and sprinkled with your own beliefs, experience, and opinions, to someone else who might feel as you do. It is trying to relate to someone a feeling or emotion and saying, you are not alone in the way that you feel. It is a way of trying to share love, hate, pain and compassion with the world.

Poetry is probably the least popular genre of books purchased today. To that end, I believe it is safe to say that neither Author of the book intends to get rich off of book sales; at least not monetarily. If some of our words could make everyone who picked it up feel good they did, that would be the greatest reward of all for us.

It is the hope of both authors that everyone who reads this book may relate personally, in some way, to some of the poems contained in this book, and know that they are not alone in their feelings. Whether good feelings, or bad, the intent of this book of poetry is to let others know that their feelings are genuine, real, and they are not alone in the way they perceive any given situation. That there are others who share the same feelings that they do; and for better or worse, no one has to endure or suffer alone, nor keep quiet their feelings of success and victory. We all share common threads of emotions and are all lifted up by hearing of someone else's experiences; both successes and failures. Each of us has something to share, something we can relate to, and something of ourselves that we can pass along to others to make the road they are traveling on a little smoother than the person who went before them.

We all indeed have something to share with each other. We all indeed have knowledge that someone can benefit from hearing about. It is to that end that we have composed this book of poetry and stand-alone thoughts; that someone's day may be a little bit brighter, just knowing that they are not alone in the way they are thinking or feeling.

It is our sincere hope that everyone who picks up this book might find a smile in it, or come to realize that the pain they feel, others too have felt. It is our sincere hope that any reader can open this book to any page and find something of inspiration, of hope or of empathy that will make them feel better, if even just for a moment, than they did prior to reading something from out of it.

To that end, it is our sincere desire that you feel moved by our words. It is our desire that you will feel so moved you will want to tell others about the book and how it made you feel. It is our desire, that it may even inspire you, to share what you feel in your heart, with us.

After all, everyone has a story to tell, feelings to express and thought to provoke inspired conversation with; which in the end, just makes all of us a little bit stronger and feel a little bit more connected to one another as we experience together, this so called "game of life."

Come along with us now, and simply relax and enjoy... Happy Reading!

G.L. Ewell

Crayon Hearts

"Most everything a person owns can be taken from them. However, memories and Love locked in your Heart, not a single soul can steal"
—Gordon Ewell

Section One
Poetry

BY KATHRYN PARKER

G.L. Ewell

Love Times One

"The best place in the world is in the arms of someone who will not only hold you at your best, but who will pick you up and hug you tight at your weakest moment."

—Unknown

Passion In Air

(by Kathryn Parker)

As the music plays

memories of the evening

flow over me until

I'm filled with

a passionate longing

to fall deeply

into his eyes,

drowning in the depths

of his love in mine.

Words flow

from his heart

with lyrics that caress

every single tear that falls

from the guitar players soul.

As the music plays

his passion flows over me

Passion In Air (Cont.)

like a minstrel of the night

Musicians write their

memories on silence,

our very essence the music,

everything beautiful his song.

Poetry written in air.

Angels & Clouds

(by Kathryn Parker)

She loves him more than her next breath of air.

He is the Angel behind her every smile,

that fills her soul

and entrances her spirit

with the warm glow

of summer sunshine.

When she speaks with him

her spirit soars

to a place

where time stands still.

Where they hold hands

and kiss beside a moonlit lake,

laugh and hold each other,

knowing they don't have to let go,

and happy knowing they were never planning to.

Where the crisp air of fall

Angels & Clouds (Cont.)

wraps them in warm sweaters,

and hot mugs of cider

as they hold hands and take walks

through falling leaves,

lost as they are in the changing colors.

He is the ecstasy of her

being so deeply in love

that happiness seems like a second language.

Passion and desire its first.

She continually loses herself in the music that

acquaints his soul.

Romanced by the melodies,

as the words of their love are written

so beautifully on the breath of the wind.

Their melodies awaiting them

just beyond the clouds.

In Perfect Time
(by Kathryn Parker)

You say hello and it begins again,

the overflowing of love

cascading from my heart

all the way through to my soul

until I can barely breathe.

Its then that the smiles begin,

not the kind that creep

across your face in

a slow progression,

but the one that lights up

everything inside from tip to toe

and makes you thankful just to be alive.

I clasp my two hands together

as tightly as I can

as if one was yours

and close my eyes

In Perfect Time (Cont.)

as the feelings consume me.

And just as it is everyday

I find I love you more.

The sun shines brightly

across the lawn

and the air is warm

as I stand in the doorway

listening to the birds.

"Thank you Lord"

sings from my Soul

to His ears.

and from my heart to yours.

The music swells in my soul

as I close my eyes and

get lost in the beat

as I love you rings out in perfect time.

Forgotten Melodies

(by Kathryn Parker)

The deep seated longing

as the silence settles

down around me

echoes in my heart,

and I sigh as i scroll

through our chats.

The words we've written

are beautiful,

and fill my soul

as the quiet music

begins again.

The lyrics,

the notes of our song,

resonating through my heart

cause my soul

to dance with a joy

Forgotten Melodies (Cont.)

I never even knew existed.

The melody

lingers in my heart

and I'll be glad to sing

for you

should you

ever awaken

to find

you've forgotten

the words.

Your Morning Prayer

(by Kathryn Parker)

As you head out the door

into the fresh light of a new day

take a moment to feel my prayers

and know that God is riding

right there beside you.

I prayed for some sun

to brighten your morning.

A cool breeze to keep you comfortable.

Music to enlighten your heart

and inspire your mind.

For God's blessings to

be seen through your eyes

but felt through His heart.

For His Peace to lift your Soul

And for my Love to fill your

cup to overflowing

Your Morning Prayer (Cont.)

as your music surrounds you.

As my prayers ascend to God's ears

my eyes swell with tears of joy

for the love that fills my heart,

for it's His never ending joy to be

the One who receives all our Praise.

Go With God My Love

for I know he holds you close.

Enjoy the love of friends and family

Share music, laughter,

good food and guitars

and the tunes that

make you smile.

As you head out the door

into the fresh light of a new day

The Lord will hear us as we gently say

Your Morning Prayer (Cont.)

"We love you Lord

Walk with me."

Because of His Love

(by Kathryn Parker)

I sit here,

a smile spreading across my face,

so in awe of the beauty

of an early morning sunrise,

thanking God for the magic

He instills in all of us

because of His love.

Because of His love my Darling

I can share my heart with you.

Because of His love

I can feel the beauty in your gentle touch.

Because of His love

I can feel my love swell deep within me

until it spills out

in poetry and tears,

and causes me to spend time

Because of His Love (Cont.)

on bended knee

as our love

all but overwhelms me.

And gives my day a beauty I dared not ask for.

Because of His love

we begin each fresh new day

with the breathtaking beauty

of an early morning sunrise.

Or feel the soothing peace of an ocean

at evening tide

View a mountain,

majestic in it's ever changing light.

or feel in awe by a field of flowers

covering a hillside

Because of His Love

we can say on bended knee,

Because of His Love (Cont.)

"Thank you God for loving me.

For filling each fresh new day

with a Strength and Grace

that only You can provide.

I ask You to be with the

one I Love My Lord.

Fill his spirit with Your Word,

His heart with Your Love.

His Soul with Your Peace,

and let him never forget,

how very much We Care."

A Birds Song

(by Kathryn Parker)

There is such a gentle peace

in a birds song.

His lilting voice sends out

the beauty held within his heart

without regard to who hears him,

or if anyone is listening at all.

You hold close this peace as a way of life,

giving both comfort,

strength,

and honor to your soul.

May My love help you take

the lumber of the day

and build within you a temple of peace.

Take the works of every day

and write a song

as peaceful and soothing

A Birds Song (Cont.)

as a birds song.

May it wrap itself around you

and heal your bone weary spirit,

soothe your weakened body,

and comfort you like a

warm blanket on a cold day.

There is such a gentle peace

in a birds song.

Comfort aflame inside your heart

waiting to be caressed by every

tender note that falls.

On The Boardwalk

(by Kathryn Parker)

I want a love like

the old couple on the boardwalk

that think nothing

of kissing in public,

or grabbing each other

in compromising places

as they dance to a song

that only they can hear.

They walk through their mornings

sharing hungry kisses

and sweet smiles,

taunting touches that cause

a bonfire to rage out of control

burning with a passion

that'll never burn down.

I want to hold you like springtime

On The Boardwalk (Cont.)

I want to kiss you like forever.

I want to set fire to your soul,

and make it easy for us to believe

in something as beautiful

as the rest of our lives

Within My Soul

(by Kathryn Parker)

Never allow those lips to utter

as much as the first syllable

of the word goodbye.

The tears

within my soul would fall

and I'd drown,

hand and heart

bound in anguish,

unable to breathe,

lost in life's deafening silence.

Magic Spark

(by Kathryn Parker)

It's snowing

and there's a magical

beauty about the earth,

as if it had suddenly

been covered in spun sugar

and it sparkles like crushed diamonds

in the moonlight.

That's your magic

That's your spark

and with it

you'll set fire to the stars.

Souls Intertwined

(by Kathryn Parker)

Oh my love, ...

Do you not know

that there will never come a day

where we are apart

one from the other?

That my heart could never

depart from yours

even unto death,

for our souls are

so intertwined

they share the

same heartbeat?

The sun rises and sets

in each others eyes

and our music

sings the same chorus.

Souls Intertwined (Cont.)

When I close my eyes

I can hear you breathing

i feel your kiss in the air

that brushes across my cheek,

and as the stirrings of dawn

awaken me from my slumber

a whisper falls upon my soul,

"Good Morning My Darling."

Desires now etched into our hearts

upon the scent of an autumn breeze.

Ghostly Streaks of Moonlight

(by Kathryn Parker)

I heard a song

its echoes

and my heart skipped a beat

I felt a wish

A teardrop

as they lay crying at my feet.

I felt your tears of long lost love

And knew them bittersweet.

I heard a song

It's echoes

and my heart skipped a beat

In the ghostly streaks of moonlight

I heard a song rising strong

I rushed to hear it's melodies

I followed it along

and on my journey

Ghostly Streaks of Moonlight (Cont.)

I fell into your eyes

When the music swelled

suddenly it was my own tears that cried.

For in those eyes I had felt your touch

Read the lyrics to your song

And as we listened to the sadness

I heard new lyrics growing strong

Your song now rings with laughter

Promises and Love

I hear Our song My Darling

Written with all my love.

Melody Of The Soul

(by Kathryn Parker)

A breeze blew softly through your hair

as you waved your goodbye's

and I took a deep breath

as I felt the heart aches begin again.

A lone tear slid down my face

and I rushed to wipe it away

before it coaxed another,

searching my heart for

the sound of your laughter

and smiling as it filled my heart.

You'll be there in my dreams my love.

moonlight shimmering off your hair

as it frames your face.

The light in your eyes a reflection

of the stars in the sky,

and my breath will catch

Melody Of The Soul (Cont.)

with every fiery glance.

"I love you my Darling"

I'll whisper,

too entranced to

be able to speak.

The melody of your

words is beautiful

and I feel blessed

to be held so tight

in the arms of

your beautiful soul.

Questions

(by Kathryn Parker)

Could it be something

as simple as a kiss?

Or the light in your eyes

that would help me to believe

that no one else would ever shine

as beautifully as you?

That no one else could

hold a candle to

your beautiful spirit?

Even the stars do their best

to alight the sky,

but in the end will only

twinkle and burn out,

their brilliance short lived

as your light remained long after

their time had come and gone.

Questions (Cont.)

Would it be your soul that called

me from my sleep

in the wee hours of the morning,

that awakened an aching for your touch.

Would it renew my faith

in everything that is beautiful

and as my tears fell

would you take my hand

and allow me to curl up beside you,

in the warmth of your soul,

listening as our song played

in the rhythm of the rain,

waiting to be caressed

by every tender drop that fell....?

Invisible Wings

(by Kathryn Parker)

Father God ...

As the beauty of this world

unfolds before us

please make us ever thankful

for the Angels that we see

walking upon this earth Dear Lord.

It is their touch,

their invisible wings

that envelop us,

and remind us

in their God given way,

how very beautiful your

blessings truly are.

It is their love that peers

inside our hearts

and sees the beauty deep within,

Invisible Wings (Cont.)

never failing to gift it back

when it is needed most.

Oh My Father

You are so Beautiful

Thank you for the Angels

on this earth.

Thank You for the one

You especially chose

to bless my every breath.

He is one of your own

So beautiful in his love for you

So cherished in the heart of one who

traveled a long way to

gift him his blessings

a compliment wrapped in kindness

that will never be forgotten.

Invisible Wings (Cont.)

Thank you Lord

for the Angel in my life

Walk with him and keep him safe.

He is one of your treasured best

And Oh Lord, I love him so.

Smoke Filled Eyes

(by Kathryn Parker)

She came to him

soft and warm,

her hair tumbling down

around her shoulders,

through a cloud

of sleep filled eyes

to read his pages,

lost in drowsy anticipation

of how they were going

to make her feel.

Her dreams for love

spoken of so beautifully,

wrapped their tendrils

around her heart

causing a longing

that could only be satisfied

Smoke Filled Eyes (Cont.)

by the passion of a hungry kiss,

or the fiery touch

of his hand upon her flesh.

Through smoke filled eyes

the passions arose

as she took his hand,

kissed him goodnight,

and lead him passionately into her dreams.

Country Dreams

(by Kathryn Parker)

He was the country boy with the million dollar smile.

The man with the rugged good looks

that made her fall all over herself,

feeling as clumsy as an ox

when he as much as smiled.

She was a simple girl

with simple dreams.

She was never taught to play

the games of love and loss

that others played.

Lying beside him she'd lose herself

in the quiet sound of his breathing,

or the feel of his skin on hers.

Moving with the music only they could hear.

As the endless refrain danced from his lips

so did the chorus explode from hers.

Country Dreams (Cont.)

The music of love

Lost in the strums of his old guitar.

Awakenings

(by Kathryn Parker)

She was enchanted

with his words

as they roused her

from her slumber

She poured a cup of coffee

and carried it to the window,

so happy that he waited

A cup of love sweetened

with the first kiss of sunlight.

An enchantment shared

as the world awakens.

Essence

(by Kathryn Parker)

Never in my entire life

have I ever known the Joy

I feel whenever I talk to you.

But tonight

listening to you laugh,

hearing you speak those

wonderful words that

sound almost magical

when you say them,

cause me to forget any lonely

moment I've ever had.

There's a song resounding

in my heart right now

that I've never heard before,

and I wish i was a songwriter

so I could capture the notes,

Essence (Cont.)

and listen to you play them

over and over and over again.

Oh My Darling

I've never loved you more.

And tomorrow, when I awaken,

after saying Good Morning to the Lord,

and thanking Him for awakening me

to another fresh new day,

I'll say Good Morning to you

and Smile as I realize

I love you even more.

The essence of our love is so sweet

What A Difference

(by Kathryn Parker)

The sound of your laughter.

The echo of your tears.

The beauty in your words.

The enthralling look in your eyes

that can turn night into day,

and cause my heart to trip

over itself in its

hope to be held,

even for a moment,

in your enticing gaze.

What a difference you've

made in my life.

I love the smiles that

take me by surprise

at three in the morning

and warm my heart.

What A Difference (Cont.)

Or the chuckle that appears

out of nowhere over

something we laughed

about hours ago,

and I'm so much in love

with how they make me feel.

You've left an indelible mark

on my very soul and

I love you more than

there are words to fill this page.

I'm not quite sure when you

turned my dreams

into sunshine

but I'm well aware

of the music that

accompanied the light.

His Quiet Peace

(by Kathryn Parker)

There's been a quiet peace

surrounding me today.

A love so tender,

yet so strong

that it moved my

soul to tears and

flowed down my cheeks,

as warm as the feelings

that accompanied them.

He sat beside me

as I prayed

and held my hand.

He wiped my tears

and smiled.

He comforted me and

told me not to worry.

His Quiet Peace (Cont.)

Our Precious Lord

listened as I

poured out my heart,

His Peace aflame

in His Soul,

filling me with a

newfound hope

and I prayed for Him

to pass it on to you,

so you would remember

always how very much

I love you.

How blessed we are in

the arms of our Savior

The King of our hearts.

May He fill your heart

His Quiet Peace (Cont.)

with His Peace,

May my love be a comfort

And may you find a beauty

in this day that you dared

not hope for.

And may you always be caressed

By every tender prayer we pray.

Wrapped In A Ribbon

(by Kathryn Parker)

The sun, streaming

through the window,

rested on my journal

and I smiled as I

picked it up and

started reading

your words.

I'll always see you

as a man who is

strong in spirit.

strong in heart,

with a soul that is kinder

than anyone I've ever met.

How blessed I am to

have your love.

What a gift you've given me.

Wrapped In A Ribbon (Cont.)

I'll always tuck myself in

with you at night

wrapped in a ribbon,

so when the sun

tugs at your eyelids

you'll remember

that as long as

I'm breathing

my love will be

my gift to you in return.

I'll tell you everyday

how much I love you

because I never want you to have

to reach into the reservoir

of your soul to find old

pieces of belonging.

Wrapped In A Ribbon (Cont.)

I'll leave pieces of my heart

on your pillow.

Poetry tucked away in secret,

so you'll never have

to wonder how much I care.

Your spirit travels to me

on the breath of the wind,

and as I close my

journal I feel your

kiss fall across my cheek.

The love sent on the whisper

of an evening breeze,

is penned from our hearts

upon scented writing paper.

Wings To Fly

(by Kathryn Parker)

Your breath is in my Soul

It is felt in every beat of my heart

Your love heard in every note of music

Every strum of the guitar

Every beat that's kept

by the drummer

in measured time.

Your soul resonates

through the crescendos,

amplifying the beauty of

its passionate soul.

The lyrics, your life,

wrap around me

awakening my heart

until my love is so strong

I am transported,

Wings To Fly (Cont.)

and reaching out to you

given wings to fly.

Your Spirits Song

(by Kathryn Parker)

I'd like to lose myself in you.

In the beauty of

just your eyes.

In the tranquility of

the evening star shine,

seen reflected at

the waters edge

,languid and still

as tidal pools.

Kissed through the tendrils

of a summer sky.

In your touch,

as passionate as our first kiss,

as gentle as a drop of dew

on a rose petal,

captivated by the

Your Spirits Song (Cont.)

mesmerizing beauty

of shadow and light

Your spirit has a song

and I can hear it,

playing bright to those

who can hear its lyrics.

Lend me your smile

I'll blow you a kiss.

I'm entranced by your touch.

Held spellbound by

the magic of your song.

The Gift

(by Kathryn Parker)

Every morning begins

with a breath of sunshine

Can I gift this back to you?

Take your hand

and ease your day?

I believe in you,

did i ever tell you that?

I believe in the man

that stands alone

that takes on the world

with strength and determination

that lives up to his promises

and cares for those he believes in

wanting nothing in return

but respect

kindness and an

The Gift (Cont.)

appreciation for the fact

that everything he does

is done out of God's

never ending love.

The Charm of the Music

(by Kathryn Parker)

I love the sparkle

of summer sunshine

streaming through the

leaves of the trees

Sparkling off the water

of a brilliant lake

causing us to trade

jeans for shorts

and boots for sandals

and days spent with someone

whose light shines so bright

that whenever we

think of them

a smile spreads across

our face that

we can feel in the

The Charm of the Music (Cont.)

depths of our spirit.

Where darkness becomes

a distant memory

chased away by the brilliance

of just their smile

Thank you Sunshine

for all my brilliant mornings

For all those creeping smiles

that crinkle my eyes,

chase away my tears,

and leave me thinking of you

with a lightened heart.

Your charm has magic

Your spirit has music

And I'd love it if you'd dance

The Charm of the Music (Cont.)

barefoot with me

in the summer sun.

Within The Looking Glass

(by Kathryn Parker)

I sit within the walls of an empty room

Curled up in blankets

Breathing deep as the quiet

settles down around me

There's so much I want to say to you

Reaching up and brushing the sleep from your eyes

Searching their depths for the answers to your questions

I wait to fill your every whim

And I wonder if I wouldn't know them all by heart

I listen intensely as you pour out your heart

Staring deep in your eyes as I kiss away each tear

Smiling as you fill each missing piece

With the Hope passed from all who love you

I'll even hold the looking glass

So you can see just how far you've come

Within The Looking Glass (Cont.)

Smoke filled clouds swirl up around you

As you stare at the screen

And I long for your touch

For the love

I would never have believed existed

Before I met you

Oh dear gentle Poet

Who could have possibly known

All it would take was one touch from you

to make the world

such a beautiful place

Remembering The Rain

(by Kathryn Parker)

It's raining

As I stare at the lake

Raindrops

Running through my hair

And over my breasts

Disappear inside my shirt

And my nipples are cold

The rain shines eerily through

the glow of the streetlights

And I am grateful for the quiet

And the peace it possesses

A shiver washes over me

As it soaks my clothes

Breathing deep the smell of fall in a rainstorm

Later a warm shower and shampoo

Will wash away the chill of the rain

Remembering The Rain (Cont.)

I'll enjoy a steaming mug of coffee

Wrapped up tightly in a towel

Wishing you were here

Curling up beside me

Forgetting the towel

But remembering the rain

To Be Remembered

(by Kathryn Parker)

It's your voice I hear

in the sound of the waves

lapping upon the shore

or in a quiet lilt

of the nightingale

graciously singing its heart out

to those with soul enough to listen,

Your laughter echoes in the

gentle rumblings

of distant thunder

Your smile seen

in the captivating

beauty of a morning sunrise

or in a rainbow

so bright and

full of color

To Be Remembered (Cont.)

Your wink will be seen

through the rain

that falls in the midst of

summer sunshine

Your words will be written

in the evening sunset

and read ever so softly

by the mesmerizing beauty of candlelight

Your signature set ablaze

in the brilliance of every falling star

Sands Through The Hourglass

(by Kathryn Parker)

He could be found
in her tender dreams
or in the midst of the
tears that poured
from her soul
as she read his words

He was the tender smile that,
when thought of,
would set her soul on fire

Closing her eyes
and breathing him in deeply
she felt a peace
flow over her
as all the ugliness
passed away
like the tiny
grains of sand
that slip through
the hourglass

Onset of Spring

(by Kathryn Parker)

On a sunny morning in the onset of spring
I'll stand in the doorway
listening to the birds
and think about you.

I want to give you everything

Warm infectious smiles
and raucous laughter

Soothing caresses, stolen glances
and never ending smiles

I want to make love to you with a passion
that all but takes our breath away
suddenly becoming so lost in its fire
that we can barely breathe

I want to take you out
for marvelous suppers
in favorite restaurants long forgotten
or served from the comfort of an easy chair
with warm conversation
and chosen music
for as long as the tunes hold out

I want to give you everything
because I love you.

Shared, because you all
but take my breath away

Song Of The Rain

(by Kathryn Parker)

Please take my hand my love

and don't let go.

The song we've composed

is alive in the

sound of the rain

falling on the roof,

in the echoes of the distant thunder,

in the raindrops

gushing through the down spouts,

quenching our thirsts

and replenishing our hearts

to the miracle of life.

Stay my love

for I will never let go

I believe in you,

our faith renewed

Song Of The Rain (Cont.)

in everything that's beautiful.

If you chase away my tears

I will banish yours

for I couldn't take it

if you were sad.

I'll beseech you with smiles

regal you with laughter

and fill you with dreams

that only we can share.

Walk with me

in the rain my love,

listen to the music

the song we have written

is beautiful,

it's sound playing from the symphony

of your beautiful soul.

Treasure Trove

(by Kathryn Parker)

How foolish would anyone have been

to have held your

heart in their hands

and then walked upon it

like their footprints

wouldn't hurt,

like you wouldn't bleed.

When I look upon you I see

a classic gem,

rare in beauty and clarity.

a treasure more lovely

than words could describe,

and would treat you as if

he were made of

the finest china,

carefully,

Treasure Trove (Cont.)

so you wouldn't break.

I'll polish you with my tears

and admire you with my heart

for it is their

that I keep the things

that are too beautiful for

the human eye.

The treasure trove

of the human soul.

Never Let Go

(by Kathryn Parker)

I Love You.

I love your voice.

I love the way it warms my heart

every time you say Hello.

I love the way certain words

dance over your tongue

before spilling out

into this magical accent

that entrances my heart.

I love the way every note of music

is like a magical spell

that takes you on a journey

of memories and priceless moments

that will always send your

heart to reeling

and your spirit to fly.

Never Let Go (Cont.)

I love how it's as much a

part of you as breathing.

I love how your heartbeats

are synchronized

with every single treasured note.

I love how your sticks

are strapped to your cane,

ready any time you're called

to add the beat and flavor

to your treasured friends every lead.

I love the regard you have

for treasured friends,

and the way you see each one

as someone with something

beautiful to share,

with those of us who have

Never Let Go (Cont.)

hearts enough to listen.

I love how you call me Angel.

How I'm your medicine.

And how peace and joy

are ingrained in my love

for that My Darling

will never die.

I love how God is at the

forefront of who we are,

and how we both know the

importance of His Word

and the depths of His love.

I Love who we are

when we're talking together,

but I also love

how we can be miles apart

Never Let Go (Cont.)

and I still feel as if your fingers

were curled around mine,

and how we both know it would be

half past forever before

either one of us could ever let go

Hearts On Fire

(by Kathryn Parker)

I signed off and watched

as our connection faded away,

but I just couldn't sleep.

I wanted you.

I wanted to look at you in a way

that would make your breath catch.

Touch you so passionately

your body would shiver from the feel

of your skin on mine.

Your lips pressing against me,

bringing us dangerously close

to the flames of a not so distant fire.

Caught in an explosion of fireworks

that will set fire to our eyebrows

leaving a trail of ash that flows

from the end of our fingertips

Hearts On Fire (Cont.)

down the middle of our back

until we're painfully aware

of the sparks that are flying.

Touch me my love.

Give me a lingering kiss

Allow your breath to catch.

Then watch while you

set me on fire.

Lyrics & Dreams

(by Kathryn Parker)

I haven't

seen everything

there is to see in this

wonderful world of ours,

and yet I feel I have everything

I could ever need

because I have you.

I have the magic of

Christmas morning all

wrapped up in your smile.

I have Wide eyed wonder

every time i choose to

view the world

through your eyes.

I have happiness

in something as warm as your "Hello"

Lyrics & Dreams (Cont.)

or as lasting as the rest of our lives.

My dreams come true

every time you call me

Sweetheart

and I wish to

fulfill every single one of yours.

Write me your lyrics My Love

I believe in your dreams

I believe in our love

And I'm held spellbound

by the magic of your song.

His Quiet Peace

(by Kathryn Parker)

From the first time I met you

I knew there was a

quiet grace about you

that was so beautiful.

The moral fibers that

you live by have adhered

themselves to your skin

and shine like a lamp in the reality

of who you really are,

A man who believes in Honesty

Integrity and

Character.

Who'll stand alone, before

he conforms to anyone

else's misconceptions.

Who's Faith in God

His Quiet Peace (Cont.)

is worn proudly,

and who suffers

bitter disappointment

when people think more of themselves

than of anybody else,

even more so when it comes

to someone in need.

A man who offers a lift to people

through their challenges,

and support through their disabilities.

A man who teaches us all

what it means to be a friend,

and has shown me everyday

what true love is all about.

Through it all you have

enchanted my spirit,

His Quiet Peace (Cont.)

embraced my soul,

and every day I fall deeper in love

with the beauty that is you.

Magical

(by Kathryn Parker)

You were just here

and I smile as I read

over your words,

glowing as the feelings begin again.

Snuggling down into its warmth

I melt into the peaceful joy that

settles gently into my soul.

"I Love You"

I can feel it in my eyes

I can feel it in my fingertips

I can hear it in the

pounding of my heart,

and in every resounding

note of music

that echoes from my soul.

Never have I known such peace

Magical (Cont.)

Never has anyone

brought me such joy

You were right My Darling,

this love is truly magical.

Kissed By Angels

(by Kathryn Parker)

My Darling,

As sure as there are stars in the sky

I know I could never let go of you.

Anything that is God orchestrated

and blessed by Angels,

is given with more love than

even we can understand.

Please don't ever tell me

that you will never bless my heart

with your beautiful smile.

That our spirits would

never again soar

from the sound of our laughter,

Sing from our hearts song,

or have our breath catch

from the touch of our lips

Kissed By Angels (Cont.)

on our skin.

Forever is much too long

to never experience the feel

of your hand in my hair,

or the feel of your lips on my skin

as you softly kiss

my tear stained cheek

with your beautiful soul.

I love you My Darling

and love is meant to be shared.

I want to give you everything.

The blessings of your love

has strengthened my life

in a way that no one else can

and what is left of our forever

would be completely impossible without you.

Loves Fire

(by Kathryn Parker)

There's a fire burning

in the yard of the house

across the street

and I marvel at its quiet beauty,

so lost in the smoke of its desires.

Let me touch you.

Let me set your soul on fire

with my deepest longing.

Capture you with a smoldering kiss.

Lick you with the flames

of my insatiable desires

Let them fly from my tongue

like the crash of a cymbal,

igniting your soul.

Love is a flame,

waiting for it to set us on fire.

Taste Of Desire

(by Kathryn Parker)

"Do you know what desire tastes like"

she asked, as the taste of a

thousand wishes traipsed off her tongue.

The warmth in his eyes

stirring a longing that

would not burn down

today,

tonight, or a thousand years from now

and she moaned as she

ached to know the taste of his lips on hers.

Desire tastes like kind touches

and sweet smiles.

Tender peace

and gentle understanding.

Blissful moans and longing

And the passion of a thousand blissful nights

Taste Of Desire (Cont.)

breathing life into his words,

"I love you"

She held them tight

knowing somewhere close

a fire had begun to smolder...

Lustful Consequence

(by Kathryn Parker)

The cat sleeps

curled up in the corner

by the window,

her paws crossed,

meowing loudly through

what has to be a

very erotic dream.

Her tail twitches every so often

adding spice to the curl on her lip

shared only with the one

with the really long whiskers

that stares at her

through the window

and is just as quickly gone

having shared both lust

and its consequence.

Lustful Consequence (Cont.)

All that was left her

was a bowl full of cream

and a nap

in order to savor

his five second love,

knowing she would

pine away lustfully

until his eventual return.

Passionate Dreams

(by Kathryn Parker)

I want to watch you sleep.

Listen to the rise and fall

of your chest as you breathe.

Feel every warm breath

every sweet smile

as you become lost

n your quiet breathing.

Your dreams of love

seen so beautifully

through sleep filled eyes.

My breath would catch

as i took your hand,

kissed you goodnight,

and led you passionately

into my dreams.

Heartbeats Of Poetry

(by Kathryn Parker)

I love your words.

Your poetry has a heartbeat.

A life all its own.

A story to tell that's beautiful.

A thought that screams to be heard.

Or perhaps an observation made,

laid between the lines,

causing your reader to think,

to draw their own conclusions.

Perhaps find something missing

from their own lives,

from their own hearts.

You paint pictures of Faith.

Your love for your fellow man,

and it's all there

in the portrait you've painted

Heartbeats Of Poetry (Cont.)

with your words

of who you are,

whether in black and white

or color,

its all there,

and I ache to read more.

You take meticulous care

in the construction of every line,

for even in poetry

every word is a lyric,

every line a song.

You're the composer

Your readers your orchestra

Your pen your baton.

Your orchestra is waiting patiently

for you to put pen to paper.

Heartbeats Of Poetry (Cont.)

Your poetry is beautiful.

If we promise to listen for a heartbeat,

wouldn't you write us another song.

The Final Rose

(by Kathryn Parker)

I took a walk in the garden

near the end of summer's bloom

to find its bed devoid of color,

searching the thorns

for what was long ago given away

and my tears fell as the leaves

gave way to thorns,

their prick as harsh

as my broken heart.

I wept deep into the night

as I headed to the water's edge,

the shadows long

by the shoreline.

It was there

in the moonlight,

the final Rose,

The Final Rose (Cont.)

and my breath caught.

The white and the pink

and I stood in awe of its beauty.

Innocence and Joy

Purity and Admiration

Chastity and Grace.

Pick it not.

Leave it to bloom

and bloom again.

Each spring will become a new beginning

of everything that is beautiful

about the world.

The air always aflame

with the intoxicating aroma of a blooming rose

Silence

(by Kathryn Parker)

I love early morning walks.

on a winter's morning,

the chill of the air

kissing my cheeks

as the silence

of the snow

settles down

around me.

You can hear

the heartbeat

of the morning

if you listen

closely enough

Handprints On The Glass

(by Kathryn Parker)

The sound of silence grew dimmer

as he sat there in the cold light of morning,

his hand pressed against the glass,

watching the clouds

as they moved across the sky.

Tears fell in his heart

as he stared out the window,

the only sound

the sound of emptiness

as his music faded away.

He looked around to spot familiar faces

and wondered if there was life beyond the glass.

"Loneliness just makes the heart grow old"

he thought as he gathered himself to meet the day.

Across the sky she stared out her window,

her hand pressed against the glass

Handprints On The Glass (Cont.)

and thought of the man with the lonely heart.

"Allow your tears to wash away

the pain in your heart gentle soul.

You have touched me with your words

and they've filled my spirit.

I believe in you and I will be there,

I promise you it won't be long.

Meanwhile my love is heard in every warm hello

and my hugs are filled with smiles.

You touched me with your tender spirit

and left me mesmerized

with the magic of stars.

And just like the handprints

we've left upon the glass,

your sparkling touch has left

an imprint on my soul."

You Were Wonderful Last Night

(by Kathryn Parker)

She smiled putting the finishing

touches on a note

left for him to read

while they were apart

one from the other

and closed her eyes,

drinking in the feelings

that caressed her heart.

His eyes languid and blue

as a summer sky.

As the water lingering

behind a waterfall

Kissed by the azure

blue of starlight

His touch, as tender as a kiss.

As soft as the whisper

You Were Wonderful Last Night (Cont.)

of his deepest secrets,

strong enough to chase

the stars from the heavens.

Or blow a memory into

the heart of her soul.

washed over her

awakening something deep inside

and she moaned in secret.

His kiss

warm

and gentle as a misty rain.

A moan heard as his lips brushed hers

or the passion aroused as their

tongues entangled.

Stirred her to her depths

The love she felt yesterday

You Were Wonderful Last Night (Cont.)

was no more than a memory.

Her love had grown,

Her desires had deepened.

You were wonderful last night My Darling.

Desires now etched in fine charcoal

upon scented writing paper.

Soft Breath of Love

(by Kathryn Parker)

It's raining

It's whisper falling softly

Upon long tangled grasses

That line the water's edge

A soft caress

Of a drop of dew in the meadow

It's kiss

Whispering your name

Within my heart

If you listen

Silence speaks

Through the unfurled wing of a meadowlark

Spanning high across a quiet lake

Through a tear slipping from your eyes

Through the deep felt longing

For a passionate kiss

Soft Breath of Love(Cont.)

By soothing lips

Brushed softly against mine

Through the reverberations of a moan

So tender it can only be heard as an echo

Hanging in the air and then gone

Like the magical flicker of a firefly

The soft breath of love

Whispers your name

I hear its calling

And my heart melts

Disappearing into the gentle touch

Of a misty rain

My kiss

Sent to you

Through the soft breath of Love

Stars In My Eyes

(by Kathryn Parker)

A cloud of smoke

surrounding us

dissipates in a breeze,

leaving no lingering trace

Lost

like a whisper in the wind.

The power of love

rushing towards the shore,

like the swell of an ocean wave,

washes over me,

its power

consuming me

and I close my eyes.

Moving into it

feeling each hug

every brush of your lips on my skin.

Stars In My Eyes (Cont.)

Blown away by its strength

amazed at

its beauty

Its warmth

allowing the intensity of it

to consume me

full to overflowing

The passion of it lingering.

The smoke of its fire

the light of the

stars in my eyes

Song Of The Soul

(by Kathryn Parker)

If you've asked me to write,

then please come hold my pen

and tell me where to start.

Reach deep into my heart

and find that place that no one

else has ever come to know.

That part of me that causes

my eyes to fill with tears

when something so beautiful

touches its spirit.

I sing to your heart

as your life spills into mine,

and I long to hear all the songs

you've written but never played.

All the dreams that belong only to you

In return I'll send you poems

Song Of The Soul (Cont.)

I've penned but never shared,

and spend years telling

you every one of mine.

Of all the roads

I've walked along,

looking for that place

where peace dwells,

to have finally found it

in your eyes,

I could never pen

anything so beautiful.

I'll sing to your spirit

as my life spills into yours,

its echoes filling our hearts like music

our spirits forever lost in our symphony's

beautiful soul.

The Notes of Your Song

(by Kathryn Parker)

In the emptiness of a quiet night

Walking through the grasses

Bare foot and peaceful

Closing my eyes

I looked up

Into the heavens

Only to see a sky

Filled with the smoke of everybody else's fire

And my breath caught

I saw a different star

And I stood transfixed

Mesmerized by its amazing beauty

A star that believes in the beauty of a caring heart

When touched by the music of an honest spirit

Believes beauty lives within

That bangles and pearls

The Notes of Your Song (Cont.)

Should be swept away

For a freshly washed face

And a gentle smile

And as I stared your song filled my heart

And I was forever changed

Shine bright Sweetheart

I hear your song

I'll hold you close in my heart

Stars as beautiful as you

Give the heavens an omnipotent beauty

And there's so much power in the notes of your song

Comin' Home

(by Kathryn Parker)

You're the one person

I wish i could

come home to.

Your warm smile

and waiting arms.

Your understanding

heart,

and a kiss

that has to be

as enticing

as my dreams.

A place where

troubles are

forced to

wait outside,

and the only

Comin' Home (Cont.)

tears allowed

to fall are

happy ones

as our peace

would never allow

a sadness.

When you say

"I love you"

it's so warm,

and it's that warmth

that I'll believe in

everyday

for the rest

of our lives,

just as I believe in You.

Your soul,

Comin' Home (Cont.)

Your heart,

Your "I love you's"

And I believe in us

in our "I love you's"

and its that love

that will always

lead me home.

The Words Of Love

(by Kathryn Parker)

I wish I could find a way to tell you

how truly beautiful I think you are.

How, with every beat of my heart

I love you more.

I ache to wrap my arms around you,

close out the world,

and show you what

true honest love is all about.

I'd spend a lifetime pouring

my heart out on sheets or paper

if I thought it would mean

you would never leave,

but in the end all I'm trying to say is

I REALLY love you,

and I ache to feel your hand in mine.

I Believe in YOU and

The Words Of Love (Cont.)

I want to share your life as it comes.

Despite what you may think

I truly wouldn't care where we were,

or what was going on around us,

or how tough you thought things were.

Don't you see,

none of that matters.

What does matter is

looking into your eyes

in the light of a fresh new day,

Joining hands and

taking on the world in peace,

we never even knew existed.

I pray there will soon come a time

when the miles between us

are no further than the feel

The Words Of Love (Cont.)

of your hand in mine.

A touch, a kiss,

soft on our faces

like the warmth

of a summer sunshine.

America's Veterans

(by Kathryn Parker)

I stood there proudly
with tears on my face,
and a lump in my chest
my hand on my heart,
the sea of white stars
lost in the sea of blue,
Red and white stripes
blowing strong in the breeze
holding tight to his hand.
His handshake
Strong
Proud
Unwavering
America's Veteran
The Pride of this Beloved Country
I felt a strength in my hand
and my chest swelled with Pride.
I was humbled by their touch
and I wondered if I could ever say
"Thank You" strongly enough
for him or her to ever known
how deeply my words went.
Those brave men and women
made the choice to
pick up a weapon,
stare the enemy in the face,
endure a hell that civilians
could never understand
and Fight for Me.
They fought
for their loved ones.

America's Veterans (Cont.)

OUR America
OUR Flag
OUR well being
OUR Rights as Americans,
and yet they never even knew me
America's Veteran.
As I stood there Proudly
tears on my face
my hand on my heart
their hand in mine,
I felt a love Like no other
and I choked back the tears
whispering a humbled Thank You
for those who mean so much
America's Veteran,
You are what makes this Country Great
and as the Flag flies proudly in the breeze
I close my eyes,
touch my hand to my heart,
and ask God to Bless you.
My love will never falter
Your Gift will never be forgotten
God Bless You ALL

What Else Could I Have Done; A Soldiers Question

(by Kathryn Parker)

The explosion sounds
And he's in battle stance
No one stands beside him
He straightens his shoulders
And searches through the scourge alone
Armor on
Weapon ready
The dust thick
The pain deep
Smoke so thick it burns
As another explosion echoes
From somewhere close beside them
And he is forced to take count
Swallowing his fear
For the sake of His Platoon
"Father why"? He screams
From somewhere deep inside
Forcing back tears
As he finds yet another fallen comrade
Taking his hand
And closing his eyes
He lifts him up
Over his shoulder
Determined no one gets left behind
He aches inside
The screaming
From somewhere undetermined
Echoing in his ears
"Father God"
"What else could I have done?"

What Else Could I Have Done; A Soldiers Question (Cont.)

The ache inside harder to take then his fear
The heart of a true Leader
Screaming
The weight of the world resting
Squarely on his shoulders
Right where he placed it
As he mourns his comrade home
The fault is NOT his own
Nothing could be done
But he won't accept it
He did not see it coming
And the whole world mourns
At the passing
Yet how many did he save?
How many lived to see the dawn?
How many walk this Earth yet today
Because of him?
How many live to bless our Lord
Watch their children grow
And remember him
With love and a deep respect?
God chooses the strong to lead his Armies
With Strength of Character
Strength of Heart
Made Strong through Faith
And love of Country
And he heeded the call
Just as his Creator knew he would
His tour of duty is over
On Foreign soil
And he came home a broken man

What Else Could I Have Done;
A Soldiers Question (Cont.)

In body
Not in Spirit
Strength of Character
Strength of Heart
Strength of Faith
Serving God
Serving Man
Ministering to the wounded
Who know his name
And are blessed by his never ending Smile
And as each day ends
And he gets down on his knees
He asks again
"Father, what else could I have done?"
God looks down smiling
"Nothing my Son
As always you have blessed my Soul"

The more I see, the less I know for sure.
— John Lennon

G.L. Ewell

Hands of Love

Section Two
Poetry

BY GORDON L. EWELL

G.L. EWELL

Love Times Two

"When you hear 'I Love You' from the one you love and get a tingle down your spine, get some 'goose bumps,' or even get giggly and tongue tied; you know for sure you are on the right path!"

—Gordon Ewell

I Thought I Knew

(by Gordon L Ewell)

I have been around the block a time or two
Learned of life from great parents, teachers and some friends too
I even learned of life from a dog named "blue"
I thought I knew about life, until I met you

I learned how to work hard, at a young age
Living free as a bird, not confined to a cage
I learned from hard knocks, even spent time in jail
For which I am thankful, for without freedom,
I then learned of hell

I have traveled the world, and seen the most unbelievable sights
It proved to me only God could paint this canvas, in six days and
nights
I learned martial arts with my cousins, how to box, how to fight
And loved to test my skills with bigger men, under many night
clubs' neon lights

In the army I deployed on "Humanitarian Missions" to help those
in need
In undeveloped countries I learned compassion, humility, and
learned to hate greed
I learned that what matters is what's in your heart
Not the size of your boat or make of your car

I met a few girls while traveling around
I thought I found love and wanted to settle down

I Thought I Knew (Cont.)

I gave them a piece of my heart, never thinking they would stomp
it right into the ground
I swore never again would I trust just to be so let down

I thought I knew life, and love until the day that we met
If someone said it would not last, I would have taken that bet
I was wrong and since then, I now believe and know there is one
Who's honest, faithful, beautiful and fun; and deserves the same
in return, all or none

I was taught to be honest, to be true; and to trust
My heart got burned too many times, and I thought had turned
to dust
I told myself never, would I do it again
Never trust someone with my heart, just to get it burned in
the end
Or at least in the past, that is what I have said
That was long before I laid a kiss upon your forehead

While spinning my wheels in false love, two princesses entered
my life
I told myself they were all that mattered, not my own heart or
absentee wife
I told myself a daddy was all I needed to be

I could be super happy, just being one of three
That was before I laid my eyes upon you; so beautiful, amazing and
honest as could be
You are the most awesome mommy on the planet
That your happy and cheerful outlook on life, even this blind man
could clearly see

I Thought I Knew (Cont.)

I was broken and busted to pieces while at war Iraq
I knew no one could ever love a broken, busted up old soldier like
that
Seven times cheated death, seven times blown to hell
Seven times fought the grim reaper, and I made him yell

I flirted with death daily in that foreign land
But I'll be damned if I would hold onto its hand
For two princesses needed me back in the states
So I busted deaths grip on me, I knew how to escape

Then home from war wounded, I knew Life no more
I found wedding vows were not binding and true friends were far
from my door
But I had two princesses that made life worth living for
They didn't see their daddy as broken, didn't understand or care
about war

They knew Daddy could not do everything quite the same as
before
They didn't care; just happy dad was home from war
That is when I knew love was not mine to be had
But I did not care because I was two princesses strongest dad of
all dads'

I told myself I would never let my heart get hurt again
For I would never expose it to anyone ever but to them
I would bury myself in the service of others, to warm my heart
It works well during the day, but the nights alone can tear you
apart

I Thought I Knew(Cont.)

Then our eyes met and my heart pounded right out of my chest
It jumped right into your car and drove off; I guess it knew what was best
When you returned, I cussed it; and told it "you'll end up a broken heart!"
But it is willing to take that chance; for it misses you too much when we are apart

I thought I knew life; did not believe in love or someone I could trust
Then along came beautiful you, on the wings of a dove
I knew then for certain, yet it was so fast and hard to believe
That true love does exists, so I let my heart stay on my sleeve

Then I got to meet, just like their mom, your amazing and wonderful kids
I immediately wanted their photos on the walls and even the fridge
I thought I knew it all; but I've never known true love and it is exciting to start
For now I know someone who is so beautiful, honest and pure of heart

Hearing Fireworks

(by Gordon L Ewell)

I heard the fireworks tonight
And was wishing I was there with you
Sitting behind you on a blanket
With your back against my chest
Or Sitting by your side
And seeing your beautiful smile
As every aerial burst lit up the sky
Just the thought of that makes me smile wide

My heart is also bursting with happiness
It is so very important in each and every way
To know where true happiness is found in life
Being able to prioritize the things that truly matter; like your
health, being an awesome parent, and friend
You share kindness, laughs and smiles with all you meet
These are just a few of the attributes which I see in you
Which I think are amazing and are so very sweet

Sometimes I wonder how you do it all
Working so hard with being everywhere for everyone
Being the best mommy and friend to all, I know leaves little time
for you
Yet I know you find much happiness in making others life
complete and worry free
A strength for all you try to be
A bright light, a guiding beacon in the night
Showing all thru your actions what is right

You make my heart pound right out of my chest
When I see your beauty radiating, and touching all those that you
know

Hearing Fireworks (Cont.)

It makes me strive to do my best as well
No matter where I go

I am honored to be your friend
I thank God for you each day
For letting me walk along the path with you
Holding hands as we walk is all my heart wants to do

Star Gazing with You

(by Gordon L Ewell)

Looking at the stars tonight

I sure seen a pretty sky

But nothing compared to the illustrious beauty,

I see within your eyes

I look to the omnipotent heaven above

And thank he who sits on the white throne on high

Not first for the alluring moonlight sky

But for being so very blessed,

To have the most beautiful woman, in you,

In my arms to share the wonders of the night

It is nights like this that we have shared

I wish would never end

But as always time seems our enemy

It never seems to want to be our friend

How I wish I could make time come to a stand

So I could have one more moment to hold your hand

Star Gazing with You (Cont.)

The time for one more kiss to steal

And with you in my arms, to place a kiss on your forehead

Time to whisper a few more words in your ear, before we leave the night sky and are off to bed

I tell myself not to be greedy too

To not wish for more than you have already blessed me with

For just One Hug and a few seconds with you

It is a priceless memory, a never ending, precious gift

Every Step of the Way

(by Gordon L Ewell)

I walked out on the back deck to look up to the breathtaking
blanket of stars above
The same blanket of diamonds of the night, under which I would
confess my love to you
To thank my lord above who created them all for such a special
night
To hold you in my strong and loving arms, ever gently, yet firm
and tight

We would sit on a swing, holding on to each other, locked in a
lovers yearning trance
Until I got the my courage up, and decided to take the chance
To open up to you, just like an open book for you to read out loud
It would be a priceless memory, it would be like sitting on a cloud

I would talk uninhibited, not shy to share my dreams of loving you
every step of the way
To kiss and enjoy one another's tender touch as lovers, yet talk like
best of friends
It would be hard to hold emotions back, as my heart said all it had
to say
Telling you of my desire to love you with faith and honor, and
never break or bend

I would hope that I could be the man, on whose chest you laid your
head upon to rest
And not foolishly promise you the moon, but rather that you
would get my very best

Every Step of the Way (Cont.)

Of everything I had to offer; my time, friendship, and all my love, would be the greatest gifts
And vow to fulfill promises to you; not give you excuses or a bunch of "buts" and "ifs"

I would have dreams of laughing and playing together, each and every day
I would "Buzz Light Year" love you; "to Infinity and beyond" is what he likes to say
It kind of a makes me laugh to say it, I know it is rather silly but it would be true
Beyond Infinity is how long, that I would love you

To go on a walk, give you a massage and hold you in my arms so tight
Oh my, it seems so wonderful, so amazing, perfect and so right
With a variety of music softly playing in low dimmed lights
Every touch would make my heart melt, to have such a perfect night

That is until the time came, if you had to go
That would just be hard, on both of us I know
But the day would come, and patient I would wait and keep in sight
The dreams of having such an amazing, meaningful, and perfect romantic life

Thinking About Love

(by Gordon L Ewell)

I may not be the smartest guy in the world...
But I would be smart enough to never lose your love

I may not be the strongest guy in the world...
But there is not a monster under a child's beds or in a closet that
I am afraid of

I may not be the wealthiest man, but would be the richest
For nothing would be more valuable than seeing the smile on your
face, and the sparkle in your eyes

I may not remember heaven; but I got a glimpse of it with you
tonight

I may not be everything to the world; but as long as I am
everything to you, that is everything to me

I thought sugar was sweet; until I tasted one of your kisses

I would think I knew what beauty was
Until I looked into your eyes

I thought I had felt love; until you took my breath away, and filled
my lungs with yours

I now know that nothing I thought I knew about love mattered;
until the day that you came into my life

Thinking About Love (Cont.)

Now everything that is anything, that is important in my life, begins and ends with you

What a wonderful thought
To have that kind of love

To be able to say goodnight to a beautiful angel
Who totally takes my breath away

And getting to say good morning to my true love
Is the most awesome way to start each day

Walk With Me

(by Gordon L Ewell)

Hold my hand
Walk with me a couple of miles
That I may have the honor of seeing
At least a dozen beautiful smiles

Let me tell you a story or two
As we walk along our path
That my ears may have the pure joy
Of listening to your incredible laugh

Let me have the honor
Of walking by your side
As we watch the beauty of a sun set
And say hello to the moon as it rises

Pause for just one moment for me
To look into your most alluring eyes
Trying to see if even one star comes close
To sparkling as bright they do, up in the vast night sky

We will tell each other many stories
About when we were kids
And laugh with each other right out loud
At some of the crazy antics that we did

Yes let me hold your hand
As we go along our walk and talk
Letting our hearts beat together happily
As we go around the block

Walk With Me (Cont.)

Let me be the first to say
How blessed I feel each and every day
For the pure love I feel for you within my heart
And of how I have felt it, right from the very start

Let me express to you
Exactly how I feel
Just like a twig off of an Acacia branch
Being carried by a beautiful Dove
A sign to me that love is true; a sign that it is real

Promises

(by Gordon L Ewell)

If I could promise you forever
And place it on your hand
Would you let me faithfully
And honorably by you stand

If I could promise you endless star-gazing nights
A forever of pure love, and never any fights
And a forever of hugs and kisses
Would you forever hold me tight

If you knew I would keep a smile upon your face
And always keep you laughing, out loud with no disgrace
Would you walk with me forever
Holding hands, and keep a steady pace

If I promised to love your kids' just like you do
And every day made time to love and play with them too
If I ensured each one of them would be successful
Would you let me help lovingly parent them with you

If I could promise the most loving family life
Full of fun and laughter and free of strife
That this world has ever known
Could I be your man and you my cherished wife

If I could promise to fix and mend your broken heart
That I would keep it whole and polished from day one
If you knew it would be my greatest treasure, and we
Would always have so much fun

Promises (Cont.)

Knowing that I would always protect it, that we
Would never come undone or grow apart
Could you find a little place for us to be together
Within a chamber of your now healing heart

I cannot promise the worlds riches
Nor worldly titles can I bestow
But I could be the most awesome lover that you could
Ever know; whose love for you would just continue to
Grow and grow
Would you let me be your loving man, if all of this I
Could prove to you and always passionately show

How Much Do I Love You

(by Gordon L Ewell)

I love you more than you could ever know Babe

How much you ask, as if seeking for a clue

Do not worry love; I would not want to see you blue

How many grains of sand, my love

On all the beaches in the world

On all the ocean floors

Take that number my love

And times it by infinity and four

How many snowflakes, my love

Make up the glacier ice packs

That cover both the north and the south poles

Take that number my love

And times it by infinity and a whole lot more

How many children do you have my love

Each I know that you adore

How Much Do I Love You (Cont.)

How much do I love you Babe

The answer is easy as can be

I will love your children with so much heart

People will think that they look a little bit like me

How much do I love you Babe

By now I think that you really don't need to ask

However I know it is fun to hear it

And I am up to the task

How much do I love thee Babe

The answerer is easy enough for me

So much that you are the only woman

I want by my side for all eternity

Eternity and an Infinite Day

(by Gordon L Ewell)

Each time you came to visit me at night
I was so excited; it was such a big delight
Just as always when I opened up the door
The very sight of you swept me right up off the floor

Once again instantly I was upon cloud nine
I could not believe this much good luck was all mine
To see you gets more magical each time I know
Because each time it's so much harder to see you go

You thought that being here at times might be a bore
To be in the same room with you, is something I adore
Time with you just cannot be anything but amazing
Just being with you anywhere will set my heart a blazing

My heart is raging with a fire that couldn't be put out
I am totally in love with you, of this there is no doubt
No doubt in my mind, my heart, or in my eye
There is no doubt to anyone that isn't blind

Holding you is the greatest thing my arms have done
It's not just passion and pleasure, it is also total fun
I can't believe I get to hold you all night long
My heart fills with so much love it could sing a song

I truly cannot imagine my life without you
I cannot imagine going even more than a day or two
If I had my way I would not go without seeing you long
But my love is not bound by time, it is so very strong

Eternity and an Infinite Day (Cont.)

To have held you and got to kiss you just one time
Thinking about it sends me right back to cloud nine
If asked how long I wanted to be yours in every way
The answer is so easy, "for eternity and an infinite day!"

A Dream Come True

(by Gordon L Ewell)

It was as if a dream came true
As I sat cross legged on the couch with you
For tonight we each spoke from our hearts
And with honesty tonight we confirmed forever starts

I dared to tell you I am so in love with you
Promises I had written down I would make come true
My heart then knew it would never again be blue
As you let me know, that you loved me too

Tonight two hearts melted into one
More beautiful than the most pastel scenic setting sun
The most amazing feeling as two hearts beat as one
As we knew beautiful, new lives had just begun

Two hearts ready to open up and let love shine bright
Hearts that felt darkness, now will be filled with light
Angels in heaven I heard cheering with such a delight
As two hearts were bonded by pure love tonight

Promises were sealed by kisses of true love
And on angel wings carried to heaven above
To be blessed by he who sits upon a throne on high
We felt our hearts on fire with his love as well tonight

Amazing feelings of love overflowed as we talked
We knew now that as one we would walk
We laughed thinking "little ones" would go with us around the block
And knew their hearts would be blessed by our love, and filled
clear to the top

A Dream Come True (Cont.)

Thoughts of our little family bound by love forever
We looked forward to a beautiful life in love together
Promises I made you from my heart
Will never be broken; knowing we will never be apart

An amazing love story just began, and become yours
As my strong arms will hold you in them forever more
It is amazing, knowing our love will last an infinite day
Knowing the last words in our book of love will say
"They lived happily ever after, every step of the way"

A Kiss Goodnight

(by Gordon L Ewell)

I watch you walk so beautiful outside at night
Gentle like a moonbeam, kissing each star in the sky
All that is most beautiful of both dark and light
I clearly see it all within your eyes
There is even a hint of pure white, like upon a dove
That I believe can only come from heaven up above

I guess the time has come for you to close them
Those beautiful alluring, take my breath away eyes
As you prepare to get some rest
Watched over by Angles from on high

Oh how I wish I could hold your hand in mine
As we say nightly prayers to our lord on high
That would be such a dream to me
I would be floating on cloud nine

For the chance to hold you close
And bed down with thee
Is something I would treasure the most
For time and all eternity

Each night I promise a big hug for you
A soft kiss on your forehead too
And in bed, one thing you can be sure of
As I hold you tight
I will never fail to gently kiss you
Before I say goodnight

Looking for the Light

(by Gordon L Ewell)

We do our best to be good people to everyone we meet
And strive to keep an eye out, for those with weary feet
Hoping we may make someone's load a little lighter
Because of our good deed, someone's day got brighter

We all hope to find someone that we can call our own
Someone very special, with whom we can build a home
We all have a dream we want to share from in our heart
We want to share it with someone special from the start

Sometimes our dreams seem impossible for us to catch
Sometimes it seems there's no one to chase them with
It may seem they get further away, like we failed a test
Like while we rested, they got away and became a myth

Often someone special comes along before our dream
And often we can't find that special one, or so it seems
That we can laugh with and love with all our heart
This seems to make our dreams unravel and fall apart

We want so desperately for our dreams to see the light
We all want so very bad, to see our dreams shine bright
Yet often it feels like our special dreams are doomed
Like we are looking for a bright light to shine on them
From the dark side of the moon

The secret is to not give up, to keep your faith and try
For giving up is the only way, that a dream can truly die

G.L. EWELL

Flower Fairy

"Never upset or worry a fairy of any kind, unless you are prepared to deal with very upset fourth and fifth grade girls."

—Gordon Ewell

Gordon L. Ewell
(Author and Poet)

Photo Courtesy of Melanie's Photoshoppe Photography

Section Three
"GORDY-ISMS"

G.L. Ewell

Love times three

"*Follow your heart. No matter what path you choose to travel, if you live, love, laugh and have a heart full of charity, willing to make time to hear, help, and love others; by following your heart, you will always end up in the right place.*"

—Gordon Ewell

The most precious "rock" or "gem-stone" in the world is not a diamond, ruby, sapphire, or even an emerald. The most precious of all, is a common old stream pebble, when handed to you with all the love in the world; by a small child who thought it so precious, that they wanted to give it to you!

Friends can make you smile and they know how to make you laugh. They pick you up when you are down, and will even borrow you a little cash. They understand your feelings, they know the real you within your heart; and they are always thinking of you, even when you are apart. They know when you are truly happy, and they know when you are blue. I thank God that there are friends who are looking out for me and you!

I would rather be a fair wind to give breath to the fire of someone else's flame, than be raging tornado that sucks the life out of it. Use caution with your words, as they have the power to be a tornado.

Like anyone else who had the weekend off and enjoyed it; I hate to see it come to an end. However, if you have a job to go to in the morning, you have a reason to be grateful, and will have a reason to enjoy your next weekend off with just as much excitement.

Smiles and Laughter have knocked down more walls than Jack Hammers, Explosives and Heavy Equipment ever will.

Sometimes failure is inevitable. However, if you have truly given 100% of yourself to your cause, there is no reason to be distraught or discouraged. Just learn from your mistakes, grow personally, and continue in your all your endeavors, putting your very best foot forward, and good things will come of it.

At the end of the day, the best and most rejuvenating sleep you will get, will start with the recollection of not what you accomplished during the day for yourself; but with what you did during the day for others who crossed your path.

Kindness is so special it was designed to be able to be delivered in many different packages: a warm smile, a gentle touch, a friendly wink of an eye, a kind word, a soft spoken voice, the wave of a hand, a kiss... No matter how you package and deliver it, kindness will always be well received.

Smiles have a unique ability to find each other. Wherever one pops up, many more are sure to follow! But don't take my word for it. Break out a smile somewhere today and just see if others smiles don't appear out of nowhere.

Ice and a cooler alone don't make a great weekend. However, when added with great friends and good music, you have a pretty good start!

The coolest thing about a genuinely happy smile is that "one size fits all!"

Only you own, operate, control and decide when, where and how to put to work one of the most powerful social tools you have... your Smile. Even under the most adverse or difficult conditions, you can put it on and almost instantly change someone's, attitude, outlook, feelings and/or state of mind. Enough of them could even change the world; at least your little corner of it

Turning your frown into a smile, is the only "U-turn" that you will never get ticketed for making.

A smile is similar to an echo, in that once you toss one out it seems to just keep going, and going, and going, and going and...

Sometimes the hardest thing for anyone to "put on" and wear with your Monday morning attire is a simple smile. However no matter how you wear it; it is sure to get noticed and inspire many other smiles in return.

Be Kind! You have the potential to make someone else's day wonderful. At worst, you could potentially have sore cheeks from smiling more than usual.
What could possibly be wrong with that?

Love is a lot like baseball, in that sometimes you have to see a few curveballs before you knock one out of the park.

Love becomes a mystery, only when people stop communicating their feelings with each other.

Good friends not only help us get through the tough times in our lives; they make life fun and fill it with laughter, joy, and just enough craziness to make it all memorable and worth it! Cherish your friends, enjoy every second of their company and companionship, and don't forget, to take the time to let them know, just how much they mean to you!

Awesome friends are like a 7-11 convenience store in that they are always available 24/7 for you and always seem to have just what you need, or need to "get you by" after midnight or "in a crunch" until everything else opens up the next day! However, to make sure you keep them available to you at any hour; make sure that you are willing to be available for them at any hour of the day as well.

Remember that more often than not, it isn't what you say that makes an impact on others as much as how you act. Most of the time your actions are having an impact the most on people you are not even aware are watching you. Let your actions speak of kindness, your words back them up, and a smile bond them together.

In the end, when it is all said and done, there are only the contents of three item of luggage you have that matter: What is in your mind; what is in your heart; and what you carry in your soul.

The best place to be in the middle of a storm, is in the arms of someone you love, or within the distance of a smile from a dear friend

No matter where you are in life, your "past" will always come knocking on your door from time to time. It is totally up to you, to decide whether to open the door, or let the "past" stay where it belongs... in the past!

Honesty comes in one form only, "Pure 100% Natural." There is no "Half-n-Half," no "Sweet –n-Lie," no "UnEqual," or "UnSplendid." The "Truth" is sweet as can be. It does not need a substitute, an exaggeration, or an alternative. It can be told "as is" and tastes great, is easily digested, and does not need to keep being added to, or stirred up. People love it poured out simply straight and bold.

No matter how many mistakes you make, no matter how many times you fall on your face, or miss a "window of opportunity;" the only thing a person ever has to worry about isn't what other people think. The only thing that you have to worry about is if you learned something... anything at all, from the mistake you made!

All tears one sheds are precious. However, the most precious of all are those that fall off your cheek, for someone other than yourself.

Often it is a person or people that you would least expect to hurt you that does you wrong. When you find that out, it hurts more than if the harm were done to you by a complete stranger. Your best reaction to their action is kindness and forgiveness when possible. When you can let it go, the hurt will go with it. As long as you hold on to it, or hold a grudge, you allow them to keep hurting you. Let it go. There will be a day that your reaction will be rewarded and their action... they will have to account for that. A day we will be glad we are not standing in their shoes!

All lies come in pairs; two for the price of one. Why? How? Because by the time you tell someone a lie, you have already told it and sold it to yourself; to enable you to tell it a second time to someone else!

This "Life" often seems unfair. That is why we have all been blessed with family, friends, and love; to help level the "playing field," and give us the "home field advantage."

One of the awesome things about great friends, is if they find out you are hurt or suffering, they will find you, no matter where you are, to lend a helping hand or be a base of support for you!

There is not a curve ball that is so perfect, that some batter has not figured how to hit out of the park, if they stay at the plate long enough!

A great way to kick off the weekend is by doing something special and unexpected for someone you love; and it could be as simple as washing their car or making them breakfast.

Some think maybe they will. Others say they "will." A few promise they will... later. A handful actually sincerely meant it when they said they would, but then called you with an excuse of why they can't. A few truly start what they said they would, and then decided the task too hard or would take too long; so, gave you an excuse and bailed on you. Then there are the precious few, who said they would, showed up on time, gave their all, and did so with a smile on their face, kept you laughing and got the job done quickly without complaining once! Take care of and return the favor for those precious few. You don't get a lot of them in your lifetime. I call them simply, "TRUE FRIENDS!"

The best way to make and keep friends is to earn their trust in you. Unfortunately, being trustworthy is not something you can just tell someone that you are. It may take some time, because trust is earned and your actions speak to others for you. Be patient and when it is earned, protect it; as if you lose someone's trust in you, hard as you may try, you may never be able to get it back.

Humility will never be found yelling, or sprouting out of anger.

The only person ever hurt by offering a hand of kindness, is the person who has never offered a hand to anyone.

Showing good manners, knowing proper customs and courtesies, and simply being polite are important! One of the simplest ways a person can be "seen in a different light" than that of their peers or co-workers is simply to be polite. Having good manners seems to be becoming a lost practice or viewed as unnecessary any more. However, if you truly want to leave an impression on someone, at a job interview, on an employer, trying to sell or market a product, with someone you are dating, or just with people in general; simply be polite and courteous. You just might be surprised at how far such a simple practice can propel you forward

Those who dare to dream and aspire to make their dreams a reality also believe in themselves and have faith to help guide them. Those who dare to let their imaginations play without borders, expand their horizons, and playfully hang on to youthful qualities that coupled with their dreams, create an environment so fertile that which is harvested is nothing less than the sweet taste of success and the humility to savor and enjoy every second of it.

You are never too young of age or heart to make mistakes; and never too old to make amends or ask for forgiveness for them.

One great thing about friends is that you will never have a shortage of them, if you simply treat them all with the same love and respect that you yourself would like to have others share with you.

Time is precious no doubt about it. Any second could be our last; or be a turning point for a re-birth or new beginning. It is all perception. But one thing about "time" is there is not enough of it to waste "time" deciding "how" you want to perceive it. If there is something you want to do, see or get out of this life, make the time now to do it; or start working toward goals you have set to achieve that which you desire to do or get out of life. Because waiting for tomorrow may just reveal that... you simply just ran out of time

People cross your path and are in your life for two reasons; either to build you up, and share their strengths, laughter, friendship and love with you, or to break you down and dump sorrow, guilt, jealousy, and hatred on you to lower your self-worth and esteem. Misery loves company, as they say. The quicker you can distance yourself from "Bad Company," the quicker you can aspire to follow your dreams and chase them without packing the weight of those who would love to hold you back. Just My Opinion... You can't soar with Eagles by hanging out with a bunch of Turkeys!

Good friends are the reason you never see just one chair at a table in a coffee shop.

Nothing in life is free. However, the very best things in life cost no more than just a little of your time, a kind word, and love.

Good friends are kind of like the small marshmallows in a cup of hot chocolate; in that it only takes a few of them bobbing in the top of your cup to get you smiling, even laughing out loud, and give your cup of coco a little something extra sweet and special in it

One key to being a good friend and liking someone for who they are; is to friend yourself and like you for who YOU are! If you can be happy with yourself, by default, everyone around you will be happy and not only feel your "Positive Vibes," but feed off of them.

When it comes the time for me to go on along down "Life's Highway," I hope I am not remembered for material wealth or a large estate; but rather by my character, and that of those I enjoyed the company of, who came to knock at my gate.

They may not travel at the speed of light, but they travel so fast, that as soon as you send one, you are receiving one back almost instantaneously! What are they? ...Smiles!

Perhaps my thinking is skewed, perhaps it is too "Old School" or "Real" for today's generation. However, I would rather tell someone the truth, even if I knew it would hurt; then tell someone a lie; even knowing that the lie may make them feel good for a moment! However, when the truth comes out (and it always will) it will hurt 100 times worse, than telling them the truth would have in that moment of time. True friends will never lie to you, even if they know the truth hurts.

As the season is changing, it reminds me that we should be changing as well. Always trying to be the best we can be. Try to add a little change into your life; like making a little time to read or meditate, or new goals to achieve in your exercise program. Make more time for those you love. Make time to visit a friend. If nothing else, remember to take the time to brush your teeth and change your underwear!

At the end of the day, when your head hits the pillow, the only person that can judge the performance of your day is you. If you can recount the day, the effort you put into it, and know others were able to smile or benefit from your actions; you can smile big and rest easy. The only person that needs to be pleased with you is you. It is you and only you that will have to look yourself in the mirror again in the morning, and like or dislike who you see looking back at you.

Sometimes the best we can do is to say "I will try again tomorrow," and not give in to discouragement.

Until one can be honest with themselves, they will never be happy or honest with others. When one is honest with themselves, it is amazing how they are not concerned with what others think of them; as they are too happy with their own life and who they are, to get caught up in the gossip and drama of what others think.

If you are fortunate to start your day laughing out loud with your best friend, until you sides hurt; I would say that is a good indication that your day is going to be an awesome one!

If you think you are right ... you probably are. If you know you are right ... there is almost no room for doubt. If you can prove you are right... there is little room for speculation. However, if you are too stubborn to listen to someone else's point of view or look at new evidence or science that could change your point of view for the better... you are WRONG! If no-one was willing to change their mind or submit to new evidence of the world around them; we would ALL still believe the world was flat!

Sometimes, even if the outcome is not exactly what you would have hoped for, it is still far better to have made a decision and acted upon it; rather than to have sat idle and done nothing at all.

Before deciding not to ease the burdens of another, perhaps we should try to "walk a mile" in their shoes.

Smiles are like a boomerang... When you throw one, it always comes back to you!

Arguments will usually produce only one of two things: enemies and hatred. However, discussions, even heated ones, based upon known truths and an individual's true feelings, can produce solutions for the common good of everyone involved in them.

Dreams are one of a very short list of things that you and only you own. Something that that there is only one original version of, something that keeps you motivated and on the right path toward your own individual happiness and one of very few things that no-one can ever take away from you; unless you allow them to!

Life will never serve us "ALL of Our Dreams" on a big Silver Platter. However, Life will serve us all a big helping of "Opportunity," to take advantage of, so that we can make our dreams come true! But is up to us to be ambitious, hardworking, and have the desire to be prepared to take a "leap of faith," and seize the moment when "Opportunity" knocks. For seldom does Life send "Opportunity" down the same street to "knock on doors" a second time!

It seem like everyone is in a big hurry anymore. We run to do this and we run to do that; but seldom do we make time to just sit and relax.

It's true that being in the right place at the right time can get you somewhere you want to be. However, when you get there, no matter how you got there, only skill, hard-work, and determination will keep you there! Take nothing for granted.

There is a very easy way to check if you are being a good listener. When someone else is talking, simply place a hand on your cheek and see if your own mouth is moving; if so, just use the same hand to close mouth and try listening again. I believe you find the result will be dramatically different and improve your listening skills 100%.

There is nothing wrong with making a mistake. It happens. What makes it wrong is if you are too full of yourself to admit you made one and try to blame others, or are not sincere and honest with yourself and learn from it; and if someone was hurt because of your actions, you fail to take ownership of them and ask for their forgiveness or understanding. Our mistakes can be some of our greatest teachers in life, if we let them be. Something else comes from bouncing back from them as well... a little thing called Character!

Responsibility and Accountability are two of the hardest traits for someone to grab ahold of and not be afraid to let others see. However, those who can embrace these traits, have a solid core of something even bigger needed for success in any endeavor... a Strong Character!

Not all clouds have a silver lining. But that's okay. How beautiful could a sunset really be, if there were but one color to paint an evening sky with?

In your every action, no matter how mundane, or where you are, you set an example for someone to observe and follow; an example for good or for bad. Whatever you do, if you can do it with a smile, chances are the example you will set for someone watching you will be a positive one. Even if you are not thrilled about what you are doing.

The most precious of all of life's treasures are not kept under lock and key. They are not guarded in Fort Knox or in a Swiss Bank under the vail of the tightest security. Where are such precious treasures in life kept, you ask of me? It is my belief they are stored in our hearts and kept on display for the whole world to see.

If you want to fill your own heart clear full with the love of someone else; one of the quickest ways is to open up your own heart and give some of its contents to others. That way there is room for someone special to give you precious pieces of their heart, for you to store in yours.

One of the very best things you can give someone is just a little bit of your heart, and of your time. I guarantee it will be one gift that they will remember the most and treasure the memory of the longest.

When you put your "best foot forward," those that matter will notice your determination to succeed. They will notice your potential for success and greater responsibilities, and your drive and motivation for success, backed by your committed heart. Those who don't will make lame comments about the brand name, style, or color of your shoes.

Live each day of your life in such a way that if anything happened to you, you would not be ashamed or embarrassed if someone wrote a book about your life. Better yet, live your life with the attitude that if someone did write a book about you, you would know that not only would it be a New York Times "Best Seller," but that it would make a positive impact on people and even change their lives for the better!

Life is too short to take it so serious you can't laugh out loud, enjoy it and have fun. Yet, it is so fragile and could be taken away at any given moment that it needs to be lived cautiously and not taken for granted. The secret to getting the most out of enjoying life is to Love and try to find a harmony and a balance between the two opposites.

A good way to end your night is with a moment on your knees, or simply with a quiet moment in your heart, giving thanks to those who were responsible for the good things that happened to come your way, to give you reason to laugh, to smile, or otherwise give you a reason to simply have a "feel good" today.

You may be the fastest thoroughbred race horse in the country. But you will never win a race if you waste your time hanging out with a heard of jackasses.

Live your life like a slow dance. Savor every detail, every soft gentle touch and movement, every soft whisper, the beat of the music, feeling love and not caring at all what anyone is thinking or saying about the way you dance. Just breathe slowly, take it all in, and enjoy the dance.

True friends are such that is does not matter if you only see them once a week, once a month, or once a year; because when you do see them the quality of the visit is such that it will carry you through until your paths cross again.

Honesty never needs further explanation. Only lies need to be re-spun, re-told, re-invented and re-hashed, over and over again.

Some of the things that matter the very most in life you cannot pull out of your wallet or your purse; like a hug, a kiss, a shoulder to cry on, a quiet moment, or a helping hand.

Everyone should seek to know their own individual limitations. That way you will know exactly where to begin to exceed them!

What matters most in life is not what we have; but rather who we have to share it with. If it were not for someone we love (a significant other, family, or friends), there is not much of anything that would be of any value to us... including memories and freedom. What we have means something, whether we have a little or a lot; because we are able to share it with others less fortunate than ourselves.

Not everyone likes cheese and wine. Some like a good well aged bourbon and a cigar. Others perhaps prefer champagne and fruit. However everyone should like and support American Farmers who grow and produce all that is needed for everything listed above; as well needed food products necessary to sustain life.

I wonder where some people seem to have gotten the idea that if you do the "right thing" and treat others with kindness and respect one day a week; that you get a "free pass" to act like an ass and lie, cheat, steal, and do things that have a negative impact on others the rest of the week? Whether you belong to an organized religion or call yourself a "Humanitarian," if you truly believe in it, you should try implementing its principals all 7 days of the week.

When self-confidence and courage, knowledge and education, hard work and determination, and faith meet at a 4-way stop on the road of one's life; nothing but success and greatness will continue thru the intersection, with happiness and joy following it.

A dear friend has a way of always making you feel your best; even if you were having a day that felt like one of your worst.

I have just one eye; yet realize you don't need eyes to see someone else's pain. You can feel it. I am legally deaf; but understand now you don't need ears to hear someone's silent cries for help. You can feel them. I can't smell very well and know you can't smell danger all the time; but you can feel it. As long as we have compassion and will trust to listen to our heart; we will be able to feel those who need a helping hand, someone to listen to them, or who could use the kindness passed along by one little smile. As long as we have a heart that cares for others; we have all we need to find those in need and fill a void with a helping hand, a kind word or deed.

Everyone has their own bag of troubles and worries to deal with. One way to make your own bag lighter is to set it down for a minute and help someone else carry their load. I guarantee when you go back to pick yours up it will not feel as heavy as it did when you set it down.

Behind every unsolicited act of kindness is a smile; that those who give of themselves for others may not show the world. However, it is a smile they wear on their heart that is so big it can warm the soul and at the end of the day, give way to a warm and peaceful sleep; no matter how cold the night or how stressful their day.

The very best of all gifts that can be given or received, begin and end with your heart.

Sometimes the best way to look into someone's heart is with your ears; by simply listening, with your own heart in tune, to what they are trying to tell you.

Some of life's most important lessons can be learned from those who have suffered and overcome adversity in their life; and had the courage and sincerity of heart to share their experiences with others. If we listen we can help ourselves. If we can relate and find the courage to do the same we can help someone else. More than likely it won't be someone you think or know you are helping; but the fact is that someone is always listening to you or watching the example you are setting. Teach them well.

Arguments are not won by seeing who can yell louder or force ones perspective on another. They are truly won when one can try to comprehend a point of view different than your own; so better communication can be had along lines of reason, to reach a common ground of understanding and agreement.

Good friends are like the wonderful taste of two scoops of your very favorite ice cream when craving a sweet snack. They are also the ambition you need to get through a rigorous exercise routine to work off those two scoops of ice cream!

You can clean your house, your garage, basement, attic; your yard and even your car. However, when you are around a child; the best thing you can clean up is your language.

If you truly want to help someone, give them your time not your opinion.

Share a smile with someone this morning. It takes longer to spell smile than it does to show one and the recipient will have a feel good that will last longer than it would take you to spell it 10,000 times!

A loving heart and compassionate mind, will always see further and understand more than the naked eye paired with an uneducated or bigoted brain.

I love the rain. I think its Mother Nature's way of washing our man-made "poop" off her front porch.

Lust has little more than the lasting brevity of a spark. Romance combines passion to give it heat and the longevity of a flame. But only true love adds a lasting friendship and compassion; to make it a fire that burns with an intensity even time cannot extinguish.

When the door to your heart opens, your arms automatically begin to reach out to those in need.

One of the best the best things you could ever do with one hand is to hold the hand of another with love.

If you truly want to have a positive impact on people with whom you cross paths with in life... spend more time worrying about how often you change your underwear, and less time gossiping and judging others.

We have eyes to see someone in need. We have ears to hear a cry for help. Our nose can smell for danger, in many ways and forms. Strong hands to work in aid of others and we have strong shoulders to carry a heavy load that may be weighing another down. Yes the blueprint of us is perfect; to fill the role of a volunteer on any given day. Perhaps best of all is a smile to share others when hard work is done and we can then stop to rest or play.

A blanket full of twinkling stars covering the sky on a moonless night is Heavens way of showing you that someone above is winking at you with love, for a kind deed, a helping hand, or even just a smile that you passed along to someone who crossed your path, and needed one, as you went about your day.

The day you quit laughing out loud, giggling at simple the silly things in life, daydreaming, using your imagination, and start acting your age and caring that others people take you serious all the time, is the day you stop being young at heart and begin to grow old.

If you want the load you are carrying to be a little lighter, try lifting it with a smile and a positive attitude.

A time to do this, a time to do that, a time to look forward, and a time to look back; a time for reflection, a time to assess, but never the time to get enough rest

If you give 100% of yourself to everything you do, to every task no matter how large or small, the worst thing anyone could say is that you did your best!

The reason pets can't talk is because God did not want us to feel constantly embarrassed by how much more common sense they have than we do.

Some say if it is meant to be it will be... I say if you want it bad enough, get off your butt and make it happen! Lack of determination, initiative and imagination is the only thing that can kill the dreams of a person with freedom!

A true warrior uses his mind and ponders how he can better himself and those around him as he hones his sword, with a love for humanity, and a heart willing to free the oppressed and fight for those who cannot fight for themselves... Not a love for brutality, but rather capable of being brutal, to protect all that he loves. That is where within his strength truly lies.

Freedom according to Webster's Dictionary is: "The state or equality of being free; being able to act, move, or use without hindrance or restraint; to choose or determine action freely; exemption of the control of some other person or some arbitrary power; Liberty; Independence; ..." of course these are a just a select few of the many definitions listed that I picked out. These are definitions that mean a lot to me. We are one of the only countries on the planet, in which we can move around our entire country without a visa, special permissions, and special papers or approving documents, anytime we choose, for any duration of time, without having to ask permission or let anyone know. We can decide at any moment to relocate anywhere in the country, and do it and any time we want without telling a sole or asking for the permission of another. We can worship as we please, speak our minds openly, own weapons to protect our families and lands from criminals who would try to deprive us of that which is ours. All this and so much more!!! In a lot of the world, a person must get permission, to even travel to a different providence, within their own country. We take so much for granted. I am honored to have served in our Armed Forces to protect the freedoms we enjoy. I have, and would spill again, my own blood, on foreign soil, protecting our freedoms. Protecting what the "Founding Fathers" of our great and mighty nation gifted us all. I would again go through the hell of war, and the hell of seven years of surgeries and therapies to get put back together again, to the best that our knowledge of medicine and science could do. However, I would like to simply ask, that sometime soon, perhaps on a weekend or while celebrating a holiday, that you will take a moment with your family, your loved ones, or your friends, to think about all the freedoms that we have and that we enjoy. Please think about the men and women who have gave their all; that we may indeed enjoy those dear to our hearts. That in peace we can treasure time with our families, children, and friends. Without fear we can attend concerts, sporting events, weekend celebrations, bar-b-ques, holidays, and anything else that we choose, in this sweet land of liberty, and do so in peace; underneath the beautiful flag of the United States of America. The only flag on earth, which represents all of these things and so much more; for each and every one of us, and to the rest of the world as well! May God Bless you all, and continue to bless the United States of America!

"Volunteers are simply Earth Angels that God does not have to continually babysit."

--Gordon L Ewell

Afterword

No matter how bad off things are for each of us, no matter what our trials or how heavy the burdens are that we shoulder, there is always someone who has it worse off than we do, and would joyfully swap their troubles for ours.

Knowing this does not make our burdens lighter. It does not make pain hurt less. It does not make financial worries disappear. That is just a plain fact! What it can do, however, from the standpoint of perspective, by reminding ourselves that it could be worse; we might just be able to find enough strength to endure one more day while we put up a fight!

By changing our perspective of how we look at our problems, we just might be able to find d new ways to deal with them... new positive ways. By just being able to have a more positive outlook on our situation's, we can indeed feel better and often see a different way of doing things that could make the way we deal with our problems, or any handicaps, or any burdens a lot easier.

Thinking of just one positive thought, or one thing to be grateful for each day and reminding ourselves of it; might just be the one thing that throughout the day, when things start to feel overwhelming, could often help to hold off a bout with the "depression monster" that usually stops by wanting ruin everyone's day at one point or another.

A positive attitude, smiles and laughter have a healing power. They certainly are not a cure-all, but they sure help.

We hope that something in the book made you laugh, or helped you understand that you are never alone, made you feel passion or loved; and most of all, for a moment, no matter how brief, took your mind off your own troubles or worries and made you smile!

We hope you will find the book a source of inspiration to you. That you might pick it up often, let it fall open on any page, and find something that inspires you and picks you up when you need a little extra boost; or gives you a smile when you are feeling a little down.

Better still, we hope that perhaps it has inspired you to think of your own positive thoughts, poems and reflections to share with us someday. Heaven knows, we need a little boost ourselves from time to time.

No one sails through their time on this spinning orb we call earth, or home, solo! At some time or another, we all need a helping hand.

If we all remembered that, and were always looking to be that helping hand for someone in need, what a totally different experience we would have. What a totally different world it would be to live in, if everyone was always looking for an opportunity to do good for someone else.

We definitely cannot change the world. However, collectively, we all have the potential to change our little corner of it for the better!

When in doubt smile!

"The Constitution was never meant to prevent people from praying; its declared purpose was to protect their freedom to pray."
—President Ronald Reagan

Kathryn Parker
(Author and Poet)

About the Author

Kathryn Parker was born in Illinois, where she discovered nature and horses, and spent most of her days lost in the depths of the woods on her horse, making memories and absorbing life. She studied Creative Writing at Gulf Park Jr. College in Mississippi. Her love of nature and horses sparked her interest in writing, but it wasn't until she had a daughter to raise alone, that she took it upon herself to further her education at University of Texas in Austin. She is a published author. She has two poetry books out, *Reflections of a Poetic Muse*, and *Poetry Within The Setting Sun*, both available at Amazon.com, as paperback and kindle books. She also has a novel in the works. Kathryn now resides in Indiana and enjoys gardening, cooking, reading, writing, horses, and her Lord and Savior Jesus Christ. Her favorite quote is, "Life is better lived with one foot hanging over the edge of insanity. A writer's soul is lost in what fills their wandering spirit, insanity whispers and they dream, and then share that with the world; their madness and their tears."

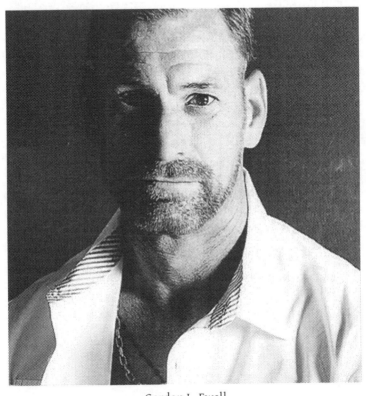

Gordon L. Ewell
(Author and Poet)

Photo Courtesy of Melanie's Photoshoppe Photography

About the Author

Gordon L. Ewell joined the National Guard after he graduated from Emery County High School in 1985. He began his military career as a radio telegraph operator, but soon decided to change course and become a Combat Engineer and demolition specialist.

During his year in Iraq, Ewell went on 59 combat missions. He led dozens of night missions looking for disguised IED's, driving five miles per hour down some of the most dangerous roadways in the country. His convoy usually contained only four or five vehicles "lit up like a Christmas tree" to shed light on potential hazards. Ewell noted that it was not unusual for his team to find 15 to18 bombs every night, and to engage with the enemy 4 or 5 times.

While deployed, Ewell started writing the Army's first route clearance handbook. Ewell's vehicle was hit by IEDs six times over the course of his deployment, including one that blew out his impacted wisdom teeth. After this explosion, Ewell was scheduled to leave to begin training another team, so he packed his mouth with gauze and caught a helicopter, only seeking medical and dental attention when he arrived at his destination. Ewell received the Bronze Star for his work as part of the first Mobile Observation Team, for writing the handbook, and for continuing to perform his route clearance duties "while engaged with the enemy."

He sustained numerous sever injuries in Iraq, which included a broken neck, severe cranial facial damage, jaw reconstruction, severe Traumatic Brain Injury, Anatomical loss of his right eye and severe hearing loss, leaving him both legally blind and deaf, severe mobility problems, neurological problems, loss of the use of his bladder, permanent nerve damage, and severe PTSD.

He was medically retired from the Army with 24 ½ years of service.

He is the Author of Four International selling books, including the highly reviewed and acclaimed book "A Lifetime at War," which received an "Eric Hoffer Award" in May 2015

He now resides in Eagle Mountain, Utah. He spends his time traveling the country doing public speaking to raise awareness for Wounded Warriors, Veterans Issues, Suicide Prevention, and Patriotism.

Noteworthy Civilian Awards

Ewell received an "Eric Hoffer Award" in the self-help category, for "Excellence in Literature" with his book "A Lifetime at War" in May 2015.

He was named, honored, and very humbled to be presented with the distinguished Myers Evergreen Memorial Park's Annual "Humanitarian of the Year" Award. The Award was presented at Myers Evergreen Memorial Park in Ogden, Utah, on May 25th, 2014.

Presented the key to the city of Leitchfield, Kentucky, by Honorable Mayor William H. Thomason on August the 12th, 2012

He was Commissioned as a "Kentucky Colonel" by the Honorable Governor Steven L. Beshear, and the Honorable Secretary of State Alison Lundergan Grimes, of the Commonwealth of Kentucky, August the 10th, 2012. It is the highest award that can be presented to a civilian by the Commonwealth of Kentucky.

Made an Honorable Duke of the city of Paducha, Kentucky by Honorable Mayor Hardy Gentry on August the 10th, 2012

Was honored to be made an Honorary Member of Rotary International, with membership in the Park City, Utah, Sunrise Club (August 15, 2011)

Selected as the Vice President of the Blue Star Riders (of Oakley, CA), Honoring and Helping our Nations Hospitalized Soldiers and their Families (September 2011)

Elected as the Senior Vice Commander of his Disabled American Veterans Section, Wasatch One, Utah. (August 03rd, 2011)

Was one of six people from Utah selected to hand stitch the Utah section onto the National 9/11 Flag that now resides at the museum at Ground Zero as a National Memorial and Treasure. (July 2011)

The State of Utah Department of Public Safety Executive Award of Merit: In recognition and appreciation of extraordinary service and outstanding contributions on behalf of the citizens of Utah (April 2008)

Presented City of Eagle Mountain Outstanding Citizenship Award (2007)

"Some people FEEL the Rain... Others just get wet!"
—Bob Marley

Kathryn Parker
(Author and Poet)

Acknowledgments from Kathryn Parker

When it came time to decide who I would like to thank for the gift I have been given to pen a few words together and form a poem, I knew the Glory had to go to my Heavenly Father. He formed me and all that is within me, and blessed me with my love for words. It states in 1st Peter 4:10 "Each one should use whatever gift he has received to serve others." Lord, thank-you for giving to me this gift of words and poetry. Thank-you for your tireless devotion to let me know, that "You Believe in ME." I pray these poems will bless your heart.

To my Mother and Father, You both loved me unconditionally and I'd like to thank them for allowing me to climb on a horse and lose myself in the wonderful forest preserve that was literally our backyard. I spent many more hours than you probably wanted me to lost on the back of my horse, exploring every nook and cranny of those woods, learning to love horses, nature, and making the memories that have influenced so much of my writing. Though you have both passed now, you never said a word on the days you happened to see me heading down the path to the woods, journal and pen in hand, knowing I would settle down on the log that had fallen across the creek, and would write until my head was clear, having locked all my problems safely in the journal that kept all my secrets.

To my brother Joe, You were, and will always remain, one of my very best friends. You supported me all of my life, were my first real friend, and loved me unconditionally. You taught me what it meant to have someone believe in me, and I will never be able to thank you enough for that. It was partly your influence that taught me to never stop reaching for the stars (May you "rest in peace").

I would be remiss if I didn't take a moment to thank my Grandmother for all the time spent sitting in the swing that hung from the ceiling on the front porch of her lake cabin. We spent many afternoons, when it was too hot to fish, talking about life, gazing out across Kentucky Lake, just happy to be together. It was her influence that made the passage through my teenage years so much easier. With her kind advice she helped me emerge in only a slightly tarnished condition, and much better equipped to handle life. I miss her very much.

To my beautiful daughter Claire, how can I even begin to say thank you strongly enough for all we have been for each other? From the minute you were born I have been in awe of what a wonderful person you are, and now that you are grown, I continue to be blown away by the absolutely amazing woman you have become. Thank you for enduring my poetry, even when it wasn't always your bag as they say, for your unconditional love, for your overwhelming support, as well as the dearest friend I could ever of asked for. I love you to the moon and back Claire. You're my Angel.

For all my friends that have stood behind me and encouraged my writing, please know that I have a very special place in my heart for you. You all are some of the greatest people anyone could have the pleasure to know, and I thank you from the bottom of my heart.

Above: Kathryn's Daughter Clair (right)

Above: Kathryn's Brother Joe (left)

Below: Kathryn's Daughter Clair

Kathryn's daughter Clair (center) and friends

Gordon L Ewell
(Public Speaking)

Photo Courtesy of Melanie's Photoshoppe Photography

Acknowledgments from Gordon Ewell

I was in the United States Military for over 24 ½ years. I would have stayed longer, but many explosions, while serving in the Global War on Terrorism, in Iraq in2006 left me severely wounded and with a long arduous 7 year recovery road in head of me. Make no mistake about it, the recovery and the many surgeries to put me back together again, as best as technology to date allows, has been hell. However, I have to admit some wonderful things have come from it as well.

I have been blessed in, that many nights of suffering with PTSD and demons has given me such empathy for so many who have went before me, to protect my freedom's, and have suffered for so long with demons of their own. Dancing with demons is hell. I get the horrible pain many of "brothers and sisters" have carried with them for so long, including my Dad, who spent over 4 years in Viet-Nam with the 1st Calvary Division. I thank you Dad; thank you to my dear Mom also, for taking care of the both of us.

I never would have done so much "deep thinking" and contemplating about life, and my place in this crazy world if it were not for so many long and lonely nights spent in hospitals, assisted living facilities, or even at home alone recovering.

I never would have begun writing seriously or doing motivational speaking if it were not for my injuries.

Trust me, it is not so great that I am about to thank the terrorists who blew me up! However, my life has become so different than it would have, had I not gotten severely injured in war.

Thank you to all those who have stood by me, and walked the walk with me down the long, long recovery road I have been on.

Thank you, to all of you who have read my thoughts, poetry, short stories, and books; and have encouraged me to keep writing. It has given me a sense of purpose.

Thank you to all my "Brothers and Sisters" who are suffering. Thank you for being "Defenders of Freedom." Know you do not suffer alone!

For everyone whose light of Patriotism shines bright, Thank you. Thank you for caring about our military service men and women, our wounded warriors, and our veterans. You can disagree with war (take that up with the government officials who start them, fund them, and commit our troops to them), and still support the brave men and women in our nation's military, and veterans who have served to protect the freedoms we enjoy and the long periods of peace we have enjoyed in our country.

I want to say thank you to my co-author Kathryn Parker. You have indeed had the patience of "Job."

Thank you to those who follow me on Facebook and other cyberspace sites, and let me know when you like my thoughts and writings or when they suck (LOL)!

Thank you to all those who are volunteers, who teach our children, who are public servants and who build our great nation up; to all those who see problems and try to fix them, all of you who indeed try to ensure America remains the greatest place on the planet to live.

From my heart, thank you to the "Higher Power" that I believe in, for being the "light in the lighthouse," that has kept my vessel from smashing into the jagged rocks that would surly have sunk me. Be a believer...

Above: Special thanks to Melanie Ewell (right) of Melanie's Photoshoppe Photography for her photos.

"*True Love is rare and often happens but once in one's lifetime. The only way to give it to someone is to show it, thru actions from the heart. Sometimes, just sometimes, the only way to show someone that pure action of true love from your heart, is to "let go" of them. No matter how much doing so hurts*".

—Gordon Ewell

All Gave Some...

G.L. EWELL

Battle Cross

...Some Gave All!

...Some Are Still Giving!

The End

Printed in the United States
By Bookmasters